Copyright (c)

All rights reserved. No part of this publication may be reproduced, distributed, or transmitted in any form or by any means, including photocopying, recording, or other electronic or mechanical methods, without the prior written permission of the publisher, except in the case of brief quotation embodied in critical reviews and certain other noncommercial uses permitted by copyright law.

Table of Contents

Introduction 3

Background and History of Gerson Therapy: 4

How Gerson Therapy Works 6

The Gerson Therapy involves a low-sodium or saltless diet to support the body's natural healing processes. 8

    Here are some tips and preparation methods for a saltless diet as part of the Gerson Therapy: 8

Nutrition plays a crucial role in healing and maintaining good health 10

    Here are some ways in which nutrition can support the healing process: 10

Following the Gerson Therapy on your Own 12

Why Are People Interested in Gerson Therapy for Cancer? 15

Tips for achieving a healthy diet that help reduce cancer risk .. 16

Meal Planning And Preparation 18

Weekly Meal Planning 27

Juicing Recipes For Gerson Diet 33

Here are recipes and their preparation methods for the Gerson Therapy diet: 40

Introduction

The Gerson Therapy diet is an alternative cancer treatment developed by Dr. Max Gerson in the 1920s. It involves a specific dietary regimen along with other complementary therapies such as coffee enemas and supplements. It is important to note that the Gerson Therapy diet is not scientifically proven or widely accepted as an effective treatment for cancer by the medical community.

The Gerson Therapy diet primarily focuses on consuming organic fruits and vegetables, particularly raw juices. The diet emphasizes the consumption of fresh, organic fruits and vegetables to provide high amounts of vitamins, minerals, and enzymes. It typically involves drinking around 13 glasses of fresh juices per day, including carrot, apple, and green leafy vegetable juices.

In addition to the juice, the Gerson Therapy diet also includes a low-sodium vegetarian diet, which includes plant-based foods such as cooked vegetables, whole grains, and legumes. It restricts the intake of salt, fats, and oils. Coffee enemas are also a key part of the therapy and are believed to aid in detoxification.

The proponents of Gerson Therapy claim that this regimen helps to boost the body's natural healing ability, detoxify the body, and strengthen the immune system to fight against cancer. However, it's important to note that there is a lack of scientific evidence supporting the effectiveness of Gerson Therapy in treating cancer, and it should not be used as a substitute for conventional medical treatments. Cancer patients should always consult with their healthcare providers and rely on evidence-based treatments.

Background and History of Gerson Therapy:

Gerson Therapy was developed by Dr. Max Gerson, a German-born physician, in the early 20th century. Dr. Gerson began his medical career specializing in internal medicine and eventually focused on developing a holistic approach to treating chronic diseases, particularly cancer.

The foundation of Gerson Therapy was established in the 1920s when Dr. Gerson started experimenting with dietary interventions to address various health conditions. He believed that toxins in the body played a significant role in the development and progression of diseases, including cancer. Based on this premise, he developed a dietary protocol aimed at detoxifying the body and supporting natural healing.

Dr. Gerson's work gained attention in the 1940s when he began treating cancer patients with his dietary approach. He reported positive outcomes and attracted both praise and controversy within the medical community. His treatment approach involved a combination of organic plant-based foods, raw juices, coffee enemas, and specific supplements to support the body's healing processes.

In the following years, Dr. Gerson and his daughter, Charlotte Gerson, continued to refine and promote Gerson Therapy. They established the Gerson Institute in the United States, which became a center for research, education, and the dissemination of information about the therapy. The Gerson Institute continues to operate today, providing information, support, and training for individuals interested in Gerson Therapy.

Over the years, Gerson Therapy has gained a dedicated following of individuals seeking alternative cancer treatments. However, it is important to note that the medical community at large does not endorse Gerson Therapy as a scientifically proven or effective treatment for cancer. The therapy has faced criticism due to a lack of rigorous scientific evidence supporting its claims and concerns about its potential risks and limitations.

Despite the controversy, Gerson Therapy remains a notable alternative treatment approach, and individuals considering it should carefully evaluate the available information, consult with healthcare professionals, and make informed decisions about their treatment options.

How Gerson Therapy Works

Gerson Therapy is based on the belief that cancer and other chronic diseases are caused by the accumulation of toxins in the body. The therapy aims to detoxify the body, boost the immune system, and promote natural healing. Here are some key principles and components of Gerson Therapy:

1. Diet: Gerson Therapy emphasizes a plant-based, organic diet. It involves consuming large amounts of fresh, organic fruits and vegetables, particularly in the form of raw juices. These juices are believed to flood the body with nutrients and enzymes, while avoiding processed foods, animal products, and fats.

2. Juicing: Freshly made juices, primarily from carrots, apples, and green leafy vegetables, are a central part of the Gerson Therapy. Patients are advised to drink up to 13 glasses of juice per day to provide high amounts of vitamins, minerals, and enzymes.

3. Coffee Enemas: Gerson Therapy incorporates the use of coffee enemas. These enemas involve the introduction of

organic, caffeinated coffee into the colon through the rectum. It is believed that coffee enemas help stimulate the liver to release toxins and promote the elimination of waste from the body.

4. Supplements: Gerson Therapy involves the use of specific supplements such as potassium, iodine, and pancreatic enzymes to support the healing process and restore nutrient levels in the body.

5. Detoxification: The therapy focuses on enhancing the body's natural detoxification mechanisms. In addition to the coffee enemas, Gerson Therapy emphasizes the importance of adequate hydration, including consuming distilled water, and using natural therapies such as castor oil packs and saunas to promote detoxification.

6. Individualization: Gerson Therapy is tailored to each individual's specific needs. It is typically administered under the guidance of a qualified Gerson practitioner who can assess the patient's condition and adjust the treatment accordingly.

The Gerson Therapy involves a low-sodium or saltless diet to support the body's natural healing processes.

Here are some tips and preparation methods for a saltless diet as part of the Gerson Therapy:

1. Avoid Processed and Packaged Foods: Processed and packaged foods often contain high amounts of sodium. It's best to eliminate or significantly reduce your consumption of these foods, including items like canned soups, snack foods, pre-packaged meals, and condiments.

2. Use Fresh Herbs and Spices: Instead of relying on salt for flavoring, incorporate fresh herbs and spices into your meals. Herbs like basil, parsley, cilantro, rosemary, and thyme, as well as spices like turmeric, cumin, paprika, and garlic powder, can add depth and flavor to your dishes.

3. Experiment with Vinegars and Citrus Juices: Vinegars (such as apple cider vinegar or balsamic vinegar) and citrus juices (like lemon or lime juice) can add tang and acidity to your meals without the need for salt. Use them as dressings for salads, marinades for proteins, or as a finishing touch to roasted vegetables.

4. Enhance Flavor with Healthy Fats: Healthy fats like olive oil, avocado oil, and coconut oil can enhance the taste and richness of your dishes. Use them for sautéing vegetables, roasting meats, or as a base for salad dressings.

5. Opt for Fresh Ingredients: Fresh fruits, vegetables, and whole grains should form the foundation of your meals. Focus on incorporating a variety of colorful produce to ensure you're getting a wide range of nutrients.

6. Experiment with Homemade Sauces and Dressings: Create your own salt-free sauces and dressings using ingredients like olive oil, vinegar, citrus juice, fresh herbs, and spices. You can find recipes online that cater to saltless diets and adapt them to your preferences.

7. Steaming and Roasting: Steaming and roasting are cooking methods that bring out the natural flavors of ingredients without the need for excessive salt. Steam vegetables until they are tender-crisp, and roast them with a drizzle of olive oil and your choice of herbs and spices.

8. Practice Mindful Eating: When following a saltless diet, it's important to focus on the flavors, textures, and aromas of the foods you consume. Take your time to savor each bite and appreciate the natural taste of the ingredients.

Nutrition plays a crucial role in healing and maintaining good health.

Here are some ways in which nutrition can support the healing process:

1. Providing Essential Nutrients: A well-balanced diet provides essential nutrients such as vitamins, minerals, proteins, carbohydrates, and fats. These nutrients are necessary for various bodily functions and are involved in processes like cell growth, tissue repair, immune function, and hormone production.

2. Supporting Immune Function: The immune system plays a vital role in defending the body against harmful pathogens and promoting healing. Proper nutrition helps strengthen the immune system by providing the necessary nutrients to produce immune cells and antibodies.

3. Reducing Inflammation: Chronic inflammation is associated with many diseases, including cancer, heart disease, and autoimmune disorders. Certain nutrients, such as omega-3 fatty acids and antioxidants found in

fruits, vegetables, and fatty fish, have anti-inflammatory properties and can help reduce inflammation in the body.

4. Promoting Tissue Repair: After an injury or illness, the body requires extra nutrients to repair damaged tissues. Protein is particularly important for tissue repair as it provides the building blocks for new cells. Including sources of high-quality protein, such as lean meats, fish, legumes, and dairy products, in the diet can support the healing process.

5. Supporting Digestive Health: The digestive system plays a crucial role in nutrient absorption and overall health. A diet rich in fiber, found in whole grains, fruits, vegetables, and legumes, promotes healthy digestion and can prevent issues such as constipation and gastrointestinal disorders.

6. Balancing Hormones: Hormonal imbalances can contribute to various health issues. Nutrients such as healthy fats, vitamin D, and zinc are important for hormone production and regulation. Including sources of these nutrients, such as avocados, nuts, seeds, fatty fish, eggs, and dairy products, can support hormonal balance.

7. Enhancing Antioxidant Defense: Antioxidants are compounds that help protect cells from damage caused by harmful molecules called free radicals. Antioxidant-rich

foods, such as berries, leafy greens, nuts, and seeds, help neutralize free radicals and reduce oxidative stress, which can contribute to chronic diseases and accelerate aging.

8. Managing Weight: Proper nutrition is essential for maintaining a healthy weight, which is important for overall health and reducing the risk of chronic diseases. A balanced diet that includes appropriate portions of nutrient-dense foods can help control appetite, provide energy, and support weight management.

Following the Gerson Therapy on your Own

Following the Gerson Therapy on your own can be challenging, as it requires strict adherence to the dietary guidelines and protocols. It's important to note that the Gerson Therapy is a specialized treatment approach for serious illnesses and should be done under the guidance of a qualified healthcare professional. However, if you are considering following a similar dietary approach for general health and well-being, here are some general guidelines to keep in mind:

1. Educate Yourself: Familiarize yourself with the principles and protocols of the Gerson Therapy. Read books, research articles, and reputable sources to gain a comprehensive understanding of the therapy's dietary guidelines, juicing protocols, and recommended supplements.

2. Seek Professional Guidance: Although following the Gerson Therapy on your own is challenging, it's recommended to consult with a qualified healthcare professional who has experience with the Gerson Therapy or similar dietary protocols. They can provide guidance, monitor your progress, and address any concerns or questions you may have.

3. Organic Produce: Emphasize the use of organic produce. Organic fruits and vegetables are free from synthetic pesticides and chemical fertilizers, which aligns with the Gerson Therapy's emphasis on a toxin-free diet. Whenever possible, choose organic options to minimize exposure to harmful substances.

4. Juicing: Juicing is a fundamental aspect of the Gerson Therapy. Invest in a good-quality juicer and follow the recommended juicing protocols. Focus on fresh, organic fruits and vegetables, such as carrots, apples, beets, and dark leafy greens. Consult resources specific to the Gerson Therapy for detailed juicing instructions and recipes.

5. Low-Sodium Vegetarian Diet: The Gerson Therapy promotes a low-sodium, vegetarian diet. Focus on consuming a variety of organic fruits, vegetables, whole grains, legumes, and nuts. Avoid processed foods, refined sugars, and added salt.

6. Meal Planning: Plan your meals in advance to ensure you have the necessary ingredients and stay on track with the dietary guidelines. Incorporate a variety of fruits, vegetables, whole grains, and plant-based proteins into your meals. Look for recipes and meal ideas that align with the Gerson Therapy's principles.

7. Supplements: The Gerson Therapy often involves the use of specific supplements, such as potassium, iodine, and pancreatic enzymes. However, the use of supplements should be done under the guidance of a healthcare professional. Consult with a qualified practitioner to determine which supplements, if any, are appropriate for your specific needs.

8. Emotional Support: Following a dietary protocol like the Gerson Therapy can be mentally and emotionally challenging. Seek support from loved ones, join support groups, or consider working with a therapist or counselor

to help navigate the emotional aspects of your healing journey.

Why Are People Interested in Gerson Therapy for Cancer?

• Hope to control the disease

Cancer is not a disease that is cured with one mode of treatment. People tend to go to any lengths and would like to try all possible treatments to get better.

Gerson therapy can cause significant complications for people and make them feel even worse.

However, changes in diet may help prevent cancer, but there is no evidence that it destroys cancer cells.

• Want to have greater control

Even though you always have control over your body, it reacts unusually and unexpectedly when with cancer.

You will resort to other types of therapy to feel accomplished.

It gives you a sense of control over your cancer and its treatment.

This should not be overlooked because willpower goes a long way.

• Boost immunity

Immunity is one of the many things that Gerson therapy may improve.

This may help fight cancer, but no scientific proof exists to support this.

Further studies are needed to establish if Gerson therapy works.

Tips for achieving a healthy diet that help reduce cancer risk

1. Fill Up on Fiber

Plant foods contain fiber, which helps remove excess hormones that could lead to certain types of cancer, including breast and prostate cancer. Fiber also helps to remove waste from the digestive system, which can play a role in preventing colorectal cancer. Eating a fiber-rich diet can also help you achieve a healthy weight, which can also help to reduce the risk for 12 types of cancer.

2. Eat the Rainbow

The more naturally colorful your diet is, the more likely it is to have an abundance of cancer-fighting compounds. The pigments that give fruits and vegetables their bright colors—like beta-carotene in sweet potatoes or lycopene in tomatoes—can help reduce cancer risk. Cruciferous vegetables, such as broccoli, kale, and cabbage, have been linked to a reduced risk of colorectal cancer, lung, and stomach cancers, while carotenoid-rich vegetables, such as carrots and sweet potatoes, have been associated with a reduced risk for breast cancer.

3. Enjoy Soy

Soy products have been associated with a reduced risk of breast cancer and a reduced risk of recurrence and mortality for women who have been previously treated for breast cancer. Research in Shanghai shows that women with breast cancer who consume 11 grams of soy protein each day can reduce mortality and risk of recurrence by about 30 percent. U.S. populations show similar findings: The higher the isoflavone intake from soy products, the less risk of mortality and recurrence in women with breast cancer.

4. Drop the Deli Meat

The World Health Organization has determined that processed meat—including deli meat, bacon, and sausage—is a major contributor to colorectal cancer, classifying it as "carcinogenic to humans." Each 50-gram daily serving of processed meat, equivalent to two slices of bacon or one sausage link, increases risk of colorectal cancer by 21%. Each 120-gram daily serving of red meat, equivalent to a small steak, increases risk of colorectal cancer by 28%.

5. Ditch the Dairy

Studies have linked high-fat dairy products to an increased risk of breast and prostate cancers. Research funded by the National Cancer Institute, the National Institutes of Health, and the World Cancer Research Fund, found that women who consumed 1/4 to 1/3 cup of cow's milk per day had a 30% increased chance for breast cancer. One cup per day increased the risk by 50%, and 2-3 cups were associated with an 80% increased chance of breast cancer. Studies have also found regular dairy consumption increases prostate cancer risk.

6. Drop the Hot Dogs

When meat is grilled, it releases carcinogens known as heterocyclic amines (HCAs), including a compound called PhIP. Studies have linked PhIP with multiple cancer. Enjoy grilling in the summer? Swap out the burgers and hot dogs for veggies, which do not produce these dangerous compounds.

7. Avoid Alcohol

Trade the cocktail for a mocktail! Drinking just one alcoholic beverage or more per day has been associated with an increased risk for colorectal cancer. Alcohol has also been linked to an increased risk for breast cancer.

Meal Planning And Preparation

Here are 50 meal planning and preparation ideas for the Gerson Therapy diet:

1. Steamed Vegetable Medley: Steam a variety of organic vegetables such as broccoli, cauliflower, carrots, and zucchini. Season with herbs and spices.

2. Brown Rice and Lentil Salad: Cook brown rice and lentils, then mix them with chopped vegetables, fresh herbs, and a lemon-tahini dressing.

3. Quinoa-Stuffed Bell Peppers: Roast bell peppers and stuff them with cooked quinoa, black beans, corn, and diced tomatoes.

4. Baked Sweet Potatoes with Steamed Greens: Bake sweet potatoes until tender and serve with a side of steamed greens like kale or Swiss chard.

5. Vegetable Stir-Fry: Stir-fry a combination of organic vegetables such as bell peppers, broccoli, snap peas, and mushrooms with a low-sodium tamari sauce.

6. Bean and Vegetable Soup: Prepare a hearty soup using a variety of beans, mixed vegetables, and vegetable broth. Season with herbs and spices.

7. Spinach and Mushroom Omelette: Make an omelette using organic eggs, sautéed spinach, mushrooms, and onions.

8. Quinoa Bowl with Roasted Vegetables: Roast a mixture of root vegetables like beets, carrots, and parsnips, and serve over cooked quinoa with a drizzle of olive oil and lemon juice.

9. Lentil Curry with Brown Rice: Cook lentils with a blend of spices and serve over brown rice for a flavorful and filling meal.

10. Mashed Cauliflower with Steamed Broccoli: Steam broccoli and serve alongside mashed cauliflower as a healthy alternative to mashed potatoes.

11. Veggie Burger with Salad: Grill or bake a homemade veggie burger and serve with a side salad of mixed greens, tomatoes, and cucumbers.

12. Zucchini Noodles with Tomato Sauce: Spiralize zucchini into noodles and top with a homemade tomato sauce made from fresh tomatoes, garlic, and herbs.

13. Black Bean Tacos with Avocado Salsa: Fill corn tortillas with seasoned black beans, and top with a fresh avocado salsa and shredded lettuce.

14. Chickpea Salad: Mix cooked chickpeas with diced cucumbers, cherry tomatoes, red onions, and a lemon-tahini dressing.

15. Stuffed Portobello Mushrooms: Fill portobello mushroom caps with a mixture of cooked quinoa, diced vegetables, and herbs. Bake until tender.

16. Ratatouille: Make a traditional ratatouille using eggplant, zucchini, bell peppers, tomatoes, and herbs. Serve over brown rice or quinoa.

17. Baked Falafel with Hummus: Bake homemade falafel patties and serve with a side of hummus and fresh vegetables.

18. Grilled Veggie Skewers: Thread skewers with a variety of grilled vegetables like bell peppers, zucchini, cherry tomatoes, and onions.

19. Lentil Bolognese with Spaghetti Squash: Cook lentils in a flavorful tomato sauce and serve over cooked spaghetti squash for a gluten-free alternative to pasta.

20. Seaweed Salad: Prepare a salad using mixed seaweed, cucumber, radishes, and a sesame-ginger dressing.

21. Stuffed Cabbage Rolls: Steam cabbage leaves and fill them with a mixture of cooked quinoa, mushrooms, and herbs. Bake until tender.

22. Greek Salad: Combine chopped cucumbers, tomatoes, red onions, olives, and feta cheese. Dress with olive oil and lemon juice.

23. Coconut Curry Vegetable Stir-Fry: Stir-fry a combination of vegetables with a coconut milk-based curry sauce. Serve over brown rice or quinoa.

24.

Chickpea and Vegetable Tagine: Cook chickpeas and a variety of vegetables in a fragrant blend of Moroccan spices. Serve over couscous.

25. Broccoli and Potato Soup: Cook a creamy soup using pureed broccoli, potatoes, onions, and vegetable broth.

26. Baked Tofu with Roasted Vegetables: Marinate tofu and roast it alongside a medley of roasted vegetables like Brussels sprouts, carrots, and red onions.

27. Spinach and Mushroom Quiche: Make a crustless quiche using organic eggs, sautéed spinach, mushrooms, onions, and dairy-free milk.

28. Greek Stuffed Peppers: Stuff bell peppers with a mixture of cooked quinoa, chopped olives, tomatoes, and herbs. Bake until tender.

29. Lentil and Vegetable Stir-Fry: Sauté cooked lentils with a variety of vegetables like bell peppers, snow peas, and carrots. Season with low-sodium tamari sauce.

30. Vegan Chili: Prepare a hearty chili using a combination of beans, diced tomatoes, onions, and spices. Serve with a side of brown rice.

31. Baked Eggplant Parmesan: Coat eggplant slices in a gluten-free breadcrumb mixture and bake until crispy. Layer with tomato sauce and dairy-free cheese.

32. Roasted Butternut Squash Soup: Roast butternut squash and blend it with vegetable broth, onions, and spices to create a creamy soup.

33. Quinoa and Vegetable Stir-Fry: Sauté cooked quinoa with a variety of vegetables like carrots, peas, and bell peppers. Season with low-sodium tamari sauce.

34. Lentil and Vegetable Curry: Cook lentils with a blend of curry spices and add a variety of vegetables like cauliflower, bell peppers, and peas.

35. Caprese Salad: Arrange sliced tomatoes, fresh basil leaves, and dairy-free mozzarella on a plate. Drizzle with balsamic glaze.

36. Stuffed Zucchini Boats: Hollow out zucchini and fill them with a mixture of cooked quinoa, diced vegetables, and herbs. Bake until tender.

37. Mediterranean Couscous Salad: Combine cooked couscous with chopped cucumbers, tomatoes, olives, red onions, and a lemon-herb dressing.

38. Sweet Potato and Black Bean Enchiladas: Fill corn tortillas with a mixture of mashed sweet potatoes, black beans, onions, and spices. Top with enchilada sauce and bake.

39. Tomato and Basil Bruschetta: Toast slices of gluten-free bread and top with diced tomatoes, fresh basil, garlic, and a drizzle of olive oil.

40. Veggie Sushi Rolls: Roll nori sheets with a combination of julienned vegetables like carrots, cucumbers, avocado, and brown rice.

41. Lentil and Vegetable Shepherd's Pie: Cook lentils with a blend of herbs and spices and layer them with mashed cauliflower or sweet potatoes.

42. Greek Stuffed Zucchini: Hollow out zucchini and stuff them with a mixture of cooked quinoa, chopped tomatoes, olives, and herbs.

43. Baked Portobello Mushroom Burger: Marinate portobello mushroom caps and bake them until tender. Serve on a gluten-free bun with toppings of choice.

44. Thai Vegetable Curry with Rice Noodles: Prepare a flavorful Thai curry using a variety of vegetables and serve over cooked rice noodles.

45. Cucumber, Tomato, and Avocado Salad: Toss sliced cucumbers, cherry tomatoes, and diced avocado with lemon juice, olive oil, and fresh herbs.

46. Lentil and Vegetable Biryani: Cook lentils and a variety of vegetables with aromatic spices and serve over basmati rice.

47. Roasted Cauliflower Steak: Slice cauliflower into thick "steaks," season with herbs and spices, and roast until golden brown.

48. Vegan Tofu Scramble: Crumble tofu and sauté it with diced vegetables, turmeric, and nutritional yeast for a vegan alternative to scrambled eggs.

49. Spaghetti Squash with Marinara Sauce: Roast spaghetti squash and top with a homemade marinara sauce and fresh herbs.

50. Baked Stuffed Mushrooms: Fill mushroom caps with a mixture of sautéed vegetables, breadcrumbs, and herbs. Bake until golden brown.

Weekly Meal Planning

Day 1:

Breakfast: Start the day off with a bowl of oatmeal, add some brown sugar, nuts, and raisins. Oatmeal is a great source of fiber and will help keep you feeling full until lunch. The nuts will give you a protein start for your day.

Snack: Try an apple with peanut butter (or any nut butters), or a handful of almonds and cheese cubes for a mid-morning snack. Keep a collection of herbal teas on hand.

Lunch: A salad made with mixed greens, cucumbers, cherry tomatoes, grilled chicken, and avocado is a perfect lunch option. Dress the salad with a homemade vinaigrette made with olive oil, balsamic vinegar, and Dijon mustard. Can't stomach a salad? Do the same thing on a sandwhich with a bit of fresh mozzarella.

Snack: Try a smoothie made with berries, Greek yogurt, peanut butter and almond milk for a great afternoon snack. Smoothies are a quick, easy, delicious way to add the nutrients you need.

Dinner: Try a grilled salmon fillet, or london broil served with roasted vegetables such as broccoli, zucchini, or sweet potato. Serve with a side of rice or quinoa.

Day 2:

Breakfast: Whip up omelet. If you're up for it, add some veggies like tomatoes or spinach, and a bit of cheese. Serve with toast.

Snack: A small cup of Greek yogurt (or vanilla yogurt) topped with sliced strawberries (or other fruit) and granola is a great mid-morning snack.

Lunch: A turkey and avocado wrap made with tortillas is a delicious and healthy lunch Add some veggies such as lettuce, tomato, and cucumber for additional nutrients.

Snack: A small handful of grapes and almonds, or a Kind Bar make for a healthy afternoon snack.

Dinner: Homemade Chicken Noodle Soups made with carrots, celery, and onions, or tasty vegetable soups are great dinner option (they also soothe a sore throat). Serve with something like these baked quesadillas (which you can fill with chicken, cheese, veggies, black beans, etc.).

Day 3:

Breakfast: A smoothie made with banana, spinach, almond milk, and vanilla protein powder is a great way to start the day.

Snack: A bowl of mixed berries, veggie sticks, or hummus and crackers are all great mid-morning snack options.

Lunch: A turkey and swiss cheese, or ham and cheese. Add some veggies such as lettuce, tomato, and cucumber for added nutrients. If you beed a change of pace, try a peanut butter and jelly sandwich.

Snack: A small handful of mixed nuts and dried fruit is a great afternoon snack. Add a glass of fruit juice.

Dinner: Try a chicken or beef stir-fry made with broccoli, carrots, peas and bell peppers. Serve with a side of rice.

Day 4:

Breakfast: Belvita Breakfast Biscuits. (They're formulated for sustainable energy and as a bonus they taste like cookies).

Snack: Baby carrots, cucumbers, grapes, or melon. Add some hummus, or yogurt to kick up the protein.

Lunch: Crockpot chicken Pot Pie Stew, a grilled chicken salad made with mixed greens, apples, mozzarella, cherry tomatoes and sliced almonds.

Snack: Trail mix, pudding or, cottage cheese topped with sliced peaches are some great afternoon snack options.

Dinner: Pasta Night. Ravioli, spaghetti, or lasagna. Add ground turkey, or lean ground beef to the sauce of your choice. Add some zucchini, or squash, or make a quick bolognese. (If you want a good jar red sauce that's not expensive, try this one...)

Day 5:

Breakfast: A slice toast and poached, hardboiled, or scrambled eggs are a good morning option.

Snack: Apple, grapes, and string cheese make for a healthy mid-morning snack.

Lunch: Tuna, chicken or egg salad sandwich, wrap, or lettuce wrap. (Add lettuce and tomatoes).

Snack: Tortilla chips and fresh guacamole.

Dinner: Grilled pork chop, shrimp, fish fillet or chicken breast served with roasted asparagus and rice is a perfect dinner option. Add a side of roasted sweet potato for added nutrients.

Day 6:

Breakfast: A bowl of Greek or vanilla yogurt topped with fruit or mixed berries and granola for a great breakfast option.

Lunch: Burrito bowl with chicken, black beans, and leftover rice. Add salsa, sour cream, or guacamole and veggies such as lettuce, tomato, cucumber for added nutrients. Sprinkle grated cheese on top.

Snack: Trail mix and dried fruit is a great afternoon snack.

Dinner: A vegetarian chili made with black beans, corn, and diced tomatoes is a great dinner option. Serve with a side of whole-grain crackers.

Day 7:

Breakfast: A smoothie made with mixed berries, Greek yogurt, and almond milk is a great way to start the day.

Snack: Fruit and string cheese, fruit salad with added granola, or cottage cheese all make for a healthy mid-morning snack.

Lunch: A grilled chicken Caesar salad made with romaine lettuce, grilled chicken, and homemade Caesar dressing is a delicious lunch option.

Snack:Trail mix, crackers and hummus, or peanut butter apples.

Dinner: Grilled salmon, London Broil, or shrimp served with roasted brussels sprouts , spinach and zucchini. Add egg noodles, rice or quinoa as a side dish.

Day 1

- Breakfast: Oatmeal with blueberries and almonds
- Lunch: Grilled chicken salad with mixed greens, cherry tomatoes, and avocado

- Dinner: Baked salmon with roasted asparagus and sweet potato

Day 2

- Breakfast: Greek yogurt with sliced banana and honey

- Lunch: Turkey and hummus wrap with cucumber and tomato

- Dinner: Beef stir-fry with broccoli, bell peppers, and brown rice

Day 3

- Breakfast: Scrambled eggs with spinach and whole wheat toast

- Lunch: Lentil soup with a side salad

- Dinner: Grilled shrimp skewers with zucchini and quinoa

Day 4

- Breakfast: Smoothie with spinach, banana, almond milk, and chia seeds

- Lunch: Tuna salad with mixed greens, cherry tomatoes, and cucumber

- Dinner: Chicken fajitas with peppers, onions, and whole wheat tortillas

Day 5

- Breakfast: Whole grain waffles with strawberries and whipped cream

- Lunch: Grilled cheese sandwich with tomato soup

- Dinner: Baked cod with roasted brussels sprouts and brown rice

Day 6

- Breakfast: Avocado toast with poached eggs and smoked salmon

- Lunch: Chicken and vegetable stir-fry with brown rice

- Dinner: Turkey chili with mixed greens and whole wheat crackers

Day 7

- Breakfast: Breakfast burrito with scrambled eggs, black beans, and salsa

- Lunch: Grilled chicken sandwich with sweet potato fries

Dinner: Baked tofu with roasted vegetables and quinoa

Juicing Recipes For Gerson Diet

1. Carrot-Apple-Ginger Juice:

   - Ingredients: Carrots, apples, ginger root

- Directions: Juice equal parts of carrots and apples, and add a small piece of ginger for added flavor.

2. Green Juice:

   - Ingredients: Kale, spinach, cucumber, green apple

   - Directions: Juice a handful of kale and spinach leaves, half a cucumber, and a green apple for a refreshing green juice.

3. Beet-Carrot-Apple Juice:

   - Ingredients: Beets, carrots, apples

   - Directions: Juice equal parts of beets, carrots, and apples for a vibrant and nutrient-rich juice.

4. Citrus Blast:

   - Ingredients: Oranges, grapefruits, lemons

   - Directions: Juice a combination of oranges, grapefruits, and lemons for a tangy and refreshing citrus juice.

5. Green-Apple-Celery Juice:

   - Ingredients: Green apples, celery, cucumber

- Directions: Juice green apples, celery stalks, and a cucumber for a hydrating and crisp green juice.

6. Pineapple-Carrot-Orange Juice:

   - Ingredients: Pineapple, carrots, oranges

   - Directions: Juice pineapple chunks, carrots, and oranges for a tropical and sweet juice.

7. Watermelon-Cucumber-Mint Juice:

   - Ingredients: Watermelon, cucumber, fresh mint leaves

   - Directions: Juice watermelon, cucumber, and add a handful of fresh mint leaves for a cooling and hydrating juice.

8. Spinach-Apple-Cucumber Juice:

   - Ingredients: Spinach, apples, cucumber

   - Directions: Juice a handful of spinach leaves, apples, and a cucumber for a nutritious and green juice.

9. Carrot-Parsley-Celery Juice:

   - Ingredients: Carrots, parsley, celery

- Directions: Juice carrots, a handful of parsley leaves, and celery stalks for a cleansing and nutrient-dense juice.

10. Red Cabbage-Apple-Lemon Juice:

   - Ingredients: Red cabbage, apples, lemon

   - Directions: Juice red cabbage, apples, and add a squeeze of lemon for a vibrant and antioxidant-rich juice.

11. Spinach-Pineapple-Celery Juice:

   - Ingredients: Spinach, pineapple, celery

   - Directions: Juice spinach, pineapple chunks, and celery stalks for a green juice with a tropical twist.

12. Carrot-Beet-Celery Juice:

   - Ingredients: Carrots, beets, celery

   - Directions: Juice carrots, beets, and celery stalks for a vibrant and earthy juice.

13. Apple-Cucumber-Mint Juice:

   - Ingredients: Apples, cucumber, fresh mint leaves

- Directions: Juice apples, cucumber, and add fresh mint leaves for a refreshing and cooling juice.

14. Kale-Pineapple-Ginger Juice:

   - Ingredients: Kale, pineapple, ginger root

   - Directions: Juice kale leaves, pineapple chunks, and a small piece of ginger for a nutrient-packed juice.

15. Carrot-Orange-Ginger-Turmeric Juice:

   - Ingredients: Carrots, oranges, ginger root, turmeric root

   - Directions: Juice carrots, oranges, ginger, and a small piece of turmeric for an immune-boosting and anti-inflammatory juice.

16. Beet-Celery-Carrot Juice:

   - Ingredients: Beets, celery, carrots

   - Directions: Juice beets, celery stalks, and carrots for a vibrant and cleansing juice.

17. Apple-Spinach-Celery Juice:

   - Ingredients:

Apples, spinach, celery

- Directions: Juice apples, spinach leaves, and celery stalks for a nutrient-dense and refreshing juice.

18. Cucumber-Parsley-Lemon Juice:

- Ingredients: Cucumber, parsley, lemon

- Directions: Juice cucumber, a handful of parsley leaves, and add a squeeze of lemon for a hydrating and cleansing juice.

19. Orange-Grapefruit-Carrot Juice:

- Ingredients: Oranges, grapefruits, carrots

- Directions: Juice oranges, grapefruits, and carrots for a tangy and vitamin-rich juice.

20. Tomato-Cucumber-Basil Juice:

- Ingredients: Tomatoes, cucumber, fresh basil leaves

- Directions: Juice tomatoes, cucumber, and add fresh basil leaves for a savory and refreshing juice.

Carrot-Apple Juice:

8-10 medium-sized carrots

2 apples (preferably Granny Smith)

Green Juice:

4-6 large green leaves (such as kale, chard, or spinach)

2-3 green apples

1 cucumber

1-2 stalks of celery

A small handful of fresh parsley

Carrot-Celery Juice:

8-10 medium-sized carrots

2-3 stalks of celery

Beet-Apple-Carrot Juice:

1 medium beet

2 apples

4-6 medium-sized carrots

Carrot-Green Leafy Juice:

8-10 medium-sized carrots

4-6 large green leaves (kale, chard, or spinach)

Here are recipes and their preparation methods for the Gerson Therapy diet:

1. Carrot-Apple-Ginger Juice:

Ingredients:

- 4-5 medium-sized carrots

- 2 apples

- 1 small piece of ginger

Preparation:

1. Wash and peel the carrots and apples.

2. Cut them into small pieces that fit your juicer.

3. Peel and chop the ginger into small chunks.

4. Juice the carrots, apples, and ginger together.

5. Stir well and serve immediately.

2. Green Vegetable Salad:

Ingredients:

- 2 cups mixed organic salad greens (spinach, kale, lettuce, etc.)

- 1 cucumber, sliced

- 1 bell pepper, sliced

- 1 tomato, diced

- 1/2 red onion, thinly sliced

- Juice of 1 lemon

- 2 tablespoons extra-virgin olive oil

- Salt and pepper to taste

Preparation:

1. In a large salad bowl, combine the salad greens, cucumber, bell pepper, tomato, and red onion.

2. In a small bowl, whisk together the lemon juice, olive oil, salt, and pepper.

3. Drizzle the dressing over the salad and toss to combine.

4. Serve immediately.

3. Steamed Vegetable Medley:

Ingredients:

- 2 cups broccoli florets

- 2 cups cauliflower florets

- 2 carrots, sliced

- 1 zucchini, sliced

- 1 tablespoon olive oil

- Herbs and spices of your choice

- Salt to taste

Preparation:

1. Place a steamer basket in a pot filled with a small amount of water.

2. Add the broccoli, cauliflower, carrots, and zucchini to the steamer basket.

3. Cover the pot and steam the vegetables for about 8-10 minutes or until tender.

4. Remove from heat and transfer the steamed vegetables to a serving bowl.

5. Drizzle with olive oil and sprinkle with herbs, spices, and salt.

6. Toss gently to coat the vegetables evenly.

7. Serve hot as a side dish.

4. Lentil and Vegetable Soup:

Ingredients:

- 1 cup dried green or brown lentils

- 1 onion, chopped

- 2 carrots, chopped

- 2 celery stalks, chopped

- 2 garlic cloves, minced

- 6 cups vegetable broth

- 1 teaspoon dried thyme

- 1 bay leaf

- Salt and pepper to taste

Preparation:

1. Rinse the lentils under cold water and set aside.

2. In a large pot, heat a little water or vegetable broth over medium heat.

3. Add the chopped onion, carrots, celery, and garlic. Sauté until vegetables are tender.

4. Add the lentils, vegetable broth, dried thyme, bay leaf, salt, and pepper.

5. Bring to a boil, then reduce heat and simmer for about 30-40 minutes, or until the lentils are cooked and tender.

6. Remove the bay leaf before serving.

7. Ladle the soup into bowls and serve hot.

5. Baked Sweet Potatoes with Steamed Greens:

Ingredients:

- 4 medium-sized sweet potatoes

- 4 cups mixed greens (kale, Swiss chard, spinach, etc.)

- 2 tablespoons extra-virgin olive oil

- 2 garlic cloves, minced

- Salt and pepper to taste

Preparation:

1. Preheat the oven to 400°F (200°C).

2. Wash the sweet potatoes and prick them with a fork.

3. Place the sweet potatoes on a baking sheet and bake for about 45-60 minutes, or until tender.

4. In

the meantime, wash and chop the mixed greens.

5. Heat the olive oil in a large skillet over medium heat.

6. Add the minced garlic and sauté for 1-2 minutes until fragrant.

7. Add the mixed greens to the skillet and sauté until wilted.

8. Season with salt and pepper to taste.

9. Once the sweet potatoes are done, remove them from the oven and let them cool slightly.

10. Slice open each sweet potato and fill with the sautéed greens.

11. Serve warm.

6. Quinoa and Vegetable Stir-Fry:

Ingredients:

- 1 cup quinoa

- 2 cups water or vegetable broth

- 2 tablespoons olive oil

- 1 onion, chopped

- 2 cloves garlic, minced

- 2 cups mixed vegetables (bell peppers, zucchini, broccoli, carrots, etc.)

- 2 tablespoons low-sodium tamari sauce or soy sauce

- Salt and pepper to taste

Preparation:

1. Rinse the quinoa thoroughly under cold water and drain.

2. In a medium saucepan, bring the water or vegetable broth to a boil.

3. Add the quinoa, reduce heat to low, cover, and simmer for about 15-20 minutes, or until all the liquid is absorbed and the quinoa is tender.

4. While the quinoa is cooking, heat the olive oil in a large skillet or wok over medium-high heat.

5. Add the chopped onion and minced garlic. Sauté until the onion is translucent and fragrant.

6. Add the mixed vegetables to the skillet and stir-fry until they are cooked but still slightly crisp.

7. Stir in the cooked quinoa and tamari sauce.

8. Season with salt and pepper to taste.

9. Cook for another 2-3 minutes, stirring continuously to combine the flavors.

10. Remove from heat and serve hot.

7. Baked Lemon Herb Salmon:

Ingredients:

- 4 salmon fillets

- Juice of 1 lemon

- 2 tablespoons fresh chopped herbs (such as dill, parsley, or basil)

- Salt and pepper to taste

Preparation:

1. Preheat the oven to 375°F (190°C).

2. Place the salmon fillets on a baking sheet lined with parchment paper.

3. Squeeze the lemon juice over the salmon.

4. Sprinkle the fresh herbs evenly over the salmon fillets.

5. Season with salt and pepper.

6. Bake in the preheated oven for about 15-20 minutes, or until the salmon is cooked through and flakes easily with a fork.

7. Serve hot with steamed vegetables or a side salad.

8. Vegetable Curry with Brown Rice:

Ingredients:

- 1 onion, chopped

- 2 cloves garlic, minced

- 1 tablespoon curry powder

- 1 teaspoon turmeric powder

- 1 teaspoon cumin powder

- 1 can (14 oz) coconut milk

- 2 cups mixed vegetables (cauliflower, bell peppers, carrots, peas, etc.)

- Salt and pepper to taste

- Cooked brown rice for serving

Preparation:

1. Heat a little water or vegetable broth in a large skillet or pot over medium heat.

2. Add the chopped onion and minced garlic. Sauté until the onion is soft and translucent.

3. Add the curry powder, turmeric powder, and cumin powder. Stir well to coat the onion and garlic with the spices.

4. Pour in the coconut milk and stir to combine.

5. Add the mixed vegetables to the skillet and stir to coat them with the curry sauce.

6. Reduce heat to low, cover, and simmer for about 15-20 minutes, or

until the vegetables are tender.

7. Season with salt and pepper to taste.

8. Serve the vegetable curry over cooked brown rice.

9. Lentil and Vegetable Stir-Fry:

Ingredients:

- 1 cup dried green or brown lentils

- 1 onion, chopped

- 2 carrots, chopped

- 2 celery stalks, chopped

- 2 garlic cloves, minced

- 6 cups vegetable broth

- 1 teaspoon dried thyme

- 1 bay leaf

- Salt and pepper to taste

Preparation:

1. Rinse the lentils under cold water and set aside.

2. In a large pot, heat a little water or vegetable broth over medium heat.

3. Add the chopped onion, carrots, celery, and garlic. Sauté until vegetables are tender.

4. Add the lentils, vegetable broth, dried thyme, bay leaf, salt, and pepper.

5. Bring to a boil, then reduce heat and simmer for about 30-40 minutes, or until the lentils are cooked and tender.

6. Remove the bay leaf before serving.

7. Ladle the soup into bowls and serve hot.

10. Mixed Berry Smoothie:

Ingredients:

- 1 cup mixed berries (strawberries, blueberries, raspberries)

- 1 ripe banana

- 1 cup almond milk (or any non-dairy milk)

- 1 tablespoon flaxseeds (ground or whole)

- 1 tablespoon almond butter

- Optional: 1 teaspoon honey or maple syrup for sweetness

Preparation:

1. Place all the ingredients in a blender.

2. Blend on high speed until smooth and creamy.

3. Taste and add honey or maple syrup if desired for extra sweetness.

4. Pour into a glass and serve immediately.

Certainly! Here are 20 recipes and their preparation methods for a cancer diet:

1. Quinoa Salad:

Ingredients:

- 1 cup cooked quinoa

- 1 cup mixed vegetables (cucumbers, cherry tomatoes, bell peppers, etc.)

- 1/4 cup chopped fresh herbs (parsley, basil, mint)

- Juice of 1 lemon

- 2 tablespoons extra-virgin olive oil

- Salt and pepper to taste

Preparation:

1. In a bowl, combine the cooked quinoa, mixed vegetables, and chopped herbs.

2. In a separate small bowl, whisk together the lemon juice, olive oil, salt, and pepper.

3. Pour the dressing over the quinoa mixture and toss to combine.

4. Serve chilled.

2. Ginger-Garlic Salmon:

Ingredients:

- 4 salmon fillets

- 2 tablespoons grated fresh ginger

- 2 cloves garlic, minced

- 2 tablespoons low-sodium soy sauce

- 1 tablespoon honey

- 1 tablespoon olive oil

Preparation:

1. Preheat the oven to 400°F (200°C).

2. In a small bowl, combine the grated ginger, minced garlic, soy sauce, honey, and olive oil.

3. Place the salmon fillets on a baking sheet lined with parchment paper.

4. Brush the ginger-garlic mixture over the salmon fillets.

5. Bake for about 12-15 minutes or until the salmon is cooked through.

6. Serve hot with steamed vegetables or brown rice.

3. Lentil Vegetable Soup:

Ingredients:

- 1 cup dried lentils (green or brown)

- 1 onion, chopped

- 2 carrots, diced

- 2 celery stalks, diced

- 2 cloves garlic, minced

- 6 cups vegetable broth

- 1 teaspoon dried thyme

- 1 bay leaf

- Salt and pepper to taste

Preparation:

1. Rinse the lentils under cold water and set aside.

2. In a large pot, sauté the chopped onion, carrots, celery, and garlic until tender.

3. Add the lentils, vegetable broth, dried thyme, bay leaf, salt, and pepper to the pot.

4. Bring to a boil, then reduce heat and simmer for about 30-40 minutes, or until the lentils are tender.

5. Remove the bay leaf before serving.

6. Ladle the soup into bowls and serve hot.

4. Grilled Chicken Breast with Roasted Vegetables:

Ingredients:

- 2 boneless, skinless chicken breasts

- 2 tablespoons olive oil

- 1 teaspoon dried herbs (such as thyme, rosemary, or oregano)

- Salt and pepper to taste

- 2 cups mixed vegetables (zucchini, bell peppers, onions, etc.)

- 1 tablespoon balsamic vinegar

Preparation:

1. Preheat the grill to medium-high heat.

2. Brush the chicken breasts with olive oil and sprinkle with dried herbs, salt, and pepper.

3. Grill the chicken for about 6-8 minutes per side, or until cooked through.

4. In the meantime, preheat the oven to 400°F (200°C).

5. Toss the mixed vegetables with olive oil, salt, and pepper.

6. Spread the vegetables on a baking sheet and roast for about 15-20 minutes, or until tender.

7. Remove the chicken from the grill and let it rest for a few minutes before slicing.

8. Drizzle the roasted vegetables with balsamic vinegar and serve alongside the grilled chicken.

5. Mediterranean Quinoa Bowl:

Ingredients:

- 1 cup cooked quinoa

- 1 cup mixed greens

- 1/2 cup cherry tomatoes, halved

- 1/4 cup chopped cucumbers

- 1/4 cup crumbled feta cheese

- 2 tablespoons sliced black olives

- 2 tablespoons extra-virgin olive oil

- Juice of 1 lemon

- Salt and pepper to taste

Preparation:

1. In a bowl, combine the cooked quinoa, mixed greens, cherry tomatoes, cucumbers, feta cheese, and black olives.

2. In a small bowl, whisk together the olive oil, lemon juice, salt, and pepper.

3. Drizzle the dressing over the quinoa mixture and toss to combine.

4. Serve chilled.

6. Roasted Butternut Squash Soup:

Ingredients:

- 1 medium butternut squash, peeled and diced

- 1 onion, chopped

- 2 carrots, chopped

- 2 cloves garlic, minced

- 4 cups vegetable broth

- 1 teaspoon dried thyme

- 1/2 teaspoon ground cinnamon

- Salt and pepper to taste

- Optional toppings: Greek yogurt, chopped fresh herbs

Preparation:

1. Preheat the oven to 400°F (200°C).

2. Place the diced butternut squash on a baking sheet and roast for about 25-30 minutes, or until tender and slightly caramelized.

3. In a large pot, sauté the chopped onion, carrots, and garlic until softened.

4. Add the roasted butternut squash, vegetable broth, dried thyme, ground cinnamon, salt, and pepper to the pot.

5. Bring to a boil, then reduce heat and simmer for about 15-20 minutes.

6. Use an immersion blender or transfer the soup to a blender to puree until smooth.

7. Adjust the seasoning if needed.

8. Ladle the soup into bowls and garnish with a dollop of Greek yogurt and chopped fresh herbs, if desired.

9. Serve hot.

7. Baked Lemon Herb Chicken:

Ingredients:

- 4 boneless, skinless chicken breasts

- Juice of 2 lemons

- 2 tablespoons fresh chopped herbs (such as rosemary, thyme, or parsley)

- 2 tablespoons olive oil

- Salt and pepper to taste

Preparation:

1. Preheat the oven to 375°F (190°C).

2. Place the chicken breasts in a baking dish.

3. Squeeze the lemon juice over the chicken.

4. Sprinkle the fresh herbs evenly over the chicken breasts.

5. Drizzle with olive oil.

6. Season with salt and pepper.

7. Bake in the preheated oven for about 25-30 minutes, or until the chicken is cooked through.

8. Serve hot with steamed vegetables or a side salad.

8. Vegetable Stir-Fry:

Ingredients:

- 2 cups mixed vegetables (broccoli, bell peppers, carrots, snap peas, etc.), sliced

- 1 tablespoon olive oil

- 2 cloves garlic, minced

- 1 tablespoon low-sodium soy sauce

- 1 tablespoon hoisin sauce (optional)

- Salt and pepper to taste

Preparation:

1. Heat the olive oil in a large skillet or wok over medium-high heat.

2. Add the minced garlic and sauté for 1-2 minutes until fragrant.

3. Add the mixed vegetables to the skillet and stir-fry for about 5-7 minutes, or until crisp-tender.

4. Stir in the soy sauce and hoisin sauce, if using.

5. Season with salt and pepper to taste.

6. Cook for another 1-2 minutes, stirring continuously.

7. Remove from heat and serve hot over

brown rice or quinoa.

9. Spinach and Mushroom Omelette:

Ingredients:

- 3 eggs

- 1/2 cup fresh spinach, chopped

- 1/4 cup sliced mushrooms

- 1/4 cup diced onions

- 1 tablespoon olive oil

- Salt and pepper to taste

Preparation:

1. In a bowl, whisk the eggs until well beaten.

2. Heat the olive oil in a non-stick skillet over medium heat.

3. Add the diced onions and sliced mushrooms to the skillet and sauté until softened.

4. Add the chopped spinach and sauté until wilted.

5. Pour the beaten eggs into the skillet, spreading them evenly to cover the vegetables.

6. Cook the omelette for a few minutes until the edges are set.

7. Gently lift the edges with a spatula and tilt the skillet to allow the uncooked eggs to flow to the edges.

8. Once the omelette is mostly set, fold it in half using the spatula.

9. Cook for another minute or two until the eggs are fully cooked and the omelette is lightly golden.

10. Season with salt and pepper.

11. Slide the omelette onto a plate and serve hot.

10. Berry Chia Pudding:

Ingredients:

- 1/2 cup mixed berries (strawberries, blueberries, raspberries)

- 2 tablespoons chia seeds

- 1 cup almond milk (or any non-dairy milk)

- 1 tablespoon honey or maple syrup (optional)

Preparation:

1. In a blender, combine the mixed berries and almond milk.

2. Blend until smooth.

3. Pour the berry mixture into a bowl or jar.

4. Stir in the chia seeds until well combined.

5. Cover and refrigerate for at least 2 hours, or until the chia seeds have absorbed the liquid and the mixture has thickened.

6. Stir the pudding well before serving.

7. If desired, drizzle with honey or maple syrup for added sweetness.

8. Enjoy chilled.

1. Roasted Vegetable Quinoa Salad:

Ingredients:

- 1 cup cooked quinoa

- 2 cups mixed roasted vegetables (such as broccoli, cauliflower, bell peppers)

- 1/4 cup chopped fresh herbs (such as parsley, basil, cilantro)

- Juice of 1 lemon

- 2 tablespoons extra-virgin olive oil

- Salt and pepper to taste

Preparation:

1. Preheat the oven to 400°F (200°C).

2. Toss the mixed vegetables with olive oil, salt, and pepper.

3. Spread the vegetables on a baking sheet and roast for about 20-25 minutes, or until tender and slightly caramelized.

4. In a bowl, combine the cooked quinoa, roasted vegetables, chopped herbs, lemon juice, olive oil, salt, and pepper.

5. Mix well to combine all the flavors.

6. Serve chilled or at room temperature.

2. Grilled Salmon with Lemon-Dill Sauce:

Ingredients:

- 4 salmon fillets

- Juice of 1 lemon

- 2 tablespoons fresh dill, chopped

- 1 tablespoon extra-virgin olive oil

- Salt and pepper to taste

Preparation:

1. Preheat the grill to medium-high heat.

2. Brush the salmon fillets with lemon juice and olive oil.

3. Sprinkle with chopped dill, salt, and pepper.

4. Grill the salmon for about 4-5 minutes per side, or until cooked through.

5. Remove from the grill and let it rest for a few minutes before serving.

6. Serve hot with a side of steamed vegetables or a green salad.

3. Quinoa Stuffed Bell Peppers:

Ingredients:

- 4 bell peppers (any color)

- 1 cup cooked quinoa

- 1/2 cup diced tomatoes

- 1/2 cup cooked black beans

- 1/4 cup chopped fresh cilantro

- 1/4 cup diced red onions

- 1/4 cup shredded mozzarella cheese (optional)

- Salt and pepper to taste

Preparation:

1. Preheat the oven to 375°F (190°C).

2. Slice off the tops of the bell peppers and remove the seeds and membranes.

3. In a bowl, combine the cooked quinoa, diced tomatoes, black beans, cilantro, red onions, salt, and pepper.

4. Spoon the quinoa mixture into the bell peppers, packing it tightly.

5. If desired, sprinkle shredded mozzarella cheese on top of each stuffed pepper.

6. Place the stuffed peppers in a baking dish and bake for about 25-30 minutes, or until the peppers are tender and the filling is heated through.

7. Remove from the oven and let them cool slightly before serving.

4. Vegetable Stir-Fry with Tofu:

Ingredients:

- 1 block of firm tofu, cubed

- 2 tablespoons low-sodium soy sauce

- 1 tablespoon cornstarch

- 2 tablespoons olive oil

- 1 cup mixed vegetables (broccoli, carrots, snap peas)

- 1 bell pepper, sliced

- 2 cloves garlic, minced

- 1 tablespoon grated fresh ginger

- 2 tablespoons low-sodium teriyaki sauce

- Salt and pepper to taste

Preparation:

1. In a bowl, toss the tofu cubes with soy sauce and cornstarch until coated.

2. Heat olive oil in a large skillet or wok over medium-high heat.

3. Add the tofu to the skillet and cook until golden brown and crispy.

4. Remove the tofu from the skillet and set aside.

5. In the same skillet, add the mixed vegetables, bell pepper, garlic, and ginger.

6. Stir-fry for about 5-7 minutes, or until the vegetables are crisp-tender.

7. Return the tofu to the skillet and add the teriyaki sauce.

8. Season with salt and pepper to taste.

9. Cook for another 2-3 minutes, stirring continuously.

10. Remove from heat and serve hot with brown rice or noodles.

5. Lentil Spinach Soup:

Ingredients:

- 1 cup dried lentils (green or brown)

- 1 onion, chopped

- 2 carrots, diced

- 2 celery stalks, diced

- 2 cloves garlic, minced

- 4 cups vegetable broth

- 2 cups fresh spinach leaves

- 1 teaspoon dried thyme

- 1 bay leaf

- Salt and pepper to taste

Preparation:

1. Rinse the lentils under cold water and set aside.

2. In a large pot, sauté the chopped onion, carrots, celery, and garlic until tender.

3. Add the lentils, vegetable broth, dried thyme, bay leaf, salt, and pepper to the pot.

4. Bring to a boil, then reduce heat and simmer for about 30-40 minutes, or until the lentils are tender.

5. Stir in the fresh spinach leaves and cook for an additional 2-3 minutes until wilted.

6. Remove the bay leaf before serving.

7. Ladle the soup into bowls and serve hot.

6. Mediterranean Chickpea Salad:

Ingredients:

- 1 can chickpeas, rinsed and drained

- 1 cup cherry tomatoes, halved

- 1 cucumber, diced

- 1/4 cup diced red onions

- 1/4 cup chopped fresh parsley

- 1/4 cup crumbled feta cheese

- Juice of 1 lemon

- 2 tablespoons extra-virgin olive oil

- Salt and pepper to taste

Preparation:

1. In a large bowl, combine the chickpeas, cherry tomatoes, cucumber, red onions, parsley, and feta cheese.

2. In a small bowl, whisk together the lemon juice, olive oil, salt, and pepper.

3. Pour the dressing over the chickpea mixture and toss to coat.

4. Let the salad marinate in the refrigerator for at least 30 minutes before serving.

5. Serve chilled.

7. Baked Chicken and Vegetable Skewers:

Ingredients:

- 2 boneless, skinless chicken breasts, cut into chunks

- 1 bell pepper, cut into chunks

- 1 zucchini, sliced

- 1 red onion, cut into chunks

- 2 tablespoons olive oil

- 1 tablespoon lemon juice

- 1 teaspoon dried herbs (such as rosemary, thyme, or oregano)

- Salt and pepper to taste

Preparation:

1. Preheat the oven to 400°F (200°C).

2. In a bowl, combine the olive oil, lemon juice, dried herbs, salt, and pepper.

3. Thread the chicken, bell pepper, zucchini, and red onion onto skewers.

4. Place the skewers on a baking sheet lined with parchment paper.

5. Brush the olive oil mixture over the skewers, coating all sides.

6. Bake in the preheated oven for about 15-20 minutes, or until the chicken is cooked through and the vegetables are tender.

7. Remove from the oven and let them cool slightly before serving.

8. Serve hot with a side of quinoa or brown rice.

8. Rainbow Vegetable Noodle Stir-Fry:

Ingredients:

- 1 zucchini

, spiralized or julienned

- 1 carrot, spiralized or julienned

- 1 bell pepper, sliced

- 1 cup snap peas

- 2 cloves garlic, minced

- 2 tablespoons low-sodium soy sauce

- 1 tablespoon sesame oil

- 1 tablespoon rice vinegar

- 1 teaspoon honey or maple syrup

- Optional toppings: sesame seeds, chopped green onions

Preparation:

1. Heat the sesame oil in a large skillet or wok over medium-high heat.

2. Add the minced garlic and sauté for 1-2 minutes until fragrant.

3. Add the spiralized zucchini, carrot, bell pepper, and snap peas to the skillet.

4. Stir-fry for about 5-7 minutes, or until the vegetables are crisp-tender.

5. In a small bowl, whisk together the soy sauce, rice vinegar, and honey.

6. Pour the sauce over the vegetable noodles and toss to coat.

7. Cook for another 1-2 minutes, stirring continuously.

8. Remove from heat and garnish with sesame seeds and chopped green onions, if desired.

9. Serve hot.

9. Berry Spinach Salad with Almonds:

Ingredients:

- 2 cups fresh spinach leaves

- 1 cup mixed berries (strawberries, blueberries, raspberries)

- 1/4 cup sliced almonds

- 2 tablespoons balsamic vinegar

- 1 tablespoon extra-virgin olive oil

- 1 teaspoon honey or maple syrup (optional)

- Salt and pepper to taste

Preparation:

1. In a large bowl, combine the fresh spinach leaves, mixed berries, and sliced almonds.

2. In a small bowl, whisk together the balsamic vinegar, olive oil, honey or maple syrup, salt, and pepper.

3. Drizzle the dressing over the salad and toss to coat.

4. Serve immediately.

10. Sweet Potato and Black Bean Chili:

Ingredients:

- 2 medium sweet potatoes, peeled and diced

- 1 onion, chopped

- 2 cloves garlic, minced

- 1 bell pepper, chopped

- 1 can black beans, rinsed and drained

- 1 can diced tomatoes

- 2 cups vegetable broth

- 2 tablespoons chili powder

- 1 teaspoon ground cumin

- 1/2 teaspoon smoked paprika

- Salt and pepper to taste

- Optional toppings: avocado, cilantro, Greek yogurt

Preparation:

1. In a large pot, sauté the chopped onion, garlic, and bell pepper until softened.

2. Add the diced sweet potatoes, black beans, diced tomatoes, vegetable broth, chili powder, cumin, smoked paprika, salt, and pepper to the pot.

3. Bring to a boil, then reduce heat and simmer for about 20-25 minutes, or until the sweet potatoes are tender.

4. Adjust the seasoning if needed.

5. Ladle the chili into bowls and top with avocado, cilantro, and a dollop of Greek yogurt, if desired.

6. Serve hot.

Printed in Great Britain
by Amazon